BRITAIN IN OLD PH

DURHAM CITY

MICHAEL F. RICHARDSON

SUTTON PUBLISHING LIMITED

Sutton Publishing Limited
Phoenix Mill · Thrupp · Stroud
Gloucestershire · GL5 2BU

First published 1996

Cover photographs: (front) Wood & Watson's entry in the Durham City Horse Parade, *c.* 1920; (back) Arthur Wilby's chimney sweep's van after an accident in North Road in June 1951.

British Library Cataloguing in Publication Data
A catalogue record for this book is available from the British Library.

ISBN 0-7509-1401-7

Typeset in 10/12 Perpetua.
Typesetting and origination by
Sutton Publishing Limited.
Printed in Great Britain by
Ebenezer Baylis, Worcester.

For Emma and Michelle

A patient customer outside the City Fish & Game Company's premises in New Elvet, 1938. To its left is the off-licence on the corner with Old Elvet, opposite the City Hotel.

Contents

Durham's most famous view, photographed by Thomas Heaviside of Queen Street (now Owengate) from the old mill below South Street, *c.* 1875. The man in the picture may be Thomas Heaviside himself. He would have had time to position himself during the lengthy exposure time then required for photographs.

INTRODUCTION

This is the third collection of old photographs of Durham put together for Sutton Publishing by Michael Richardson from his unique collection of more than three thousand items. An Australian expatriate, Andrew Eves, wrote to him about his first collection and told him about his family's life at 51 Old Elvet where his grandparents had run a boarding house in the 1940s. He remarked: 'Durham evokes extremely fond memories for me, and your book certainly encapsulates what a great city Durham is, and the people.' I have no doubt that many will feel much the same about this collection.

Durham was saved from damage in the Second World War by what seems like a small miracle. Miss Gwen Wilkinson was on fire-guard duty in the city in May 1942. One night, at about 2.40 a.m., as the sirens sounded she saw the Cathedral and Banks bathed in brilliant moonlight. But suddenly, a mist arose from the River Wear and gradually encircled the central tower of the Cathedral and ultimately all the Rock. Only then was the drone of enemy raiders heard. Not finding their target they dropped their bombs harmlessly but the Royal Observer Corps had plotted a concentrated raid converging on the city. Their identification a year before of the BF110 fighter plane which brought Rudolf Hess to Scotland, an identification which was scoffed at by Fighter Command, had proved their professional standard of training. The mist that saved Durham is now commemorated in the Cathedral's RAF memorial window by Commander Easton – as recently as the summer of 1996 when a mist arose from the river people thought that the Cathedral was on fire and called out the fire brigade.

Durham is a city blessed with many strands of continuity. The story of Archibald's – the nearest the city has to a department store – is an interesting example. It was founded in 1840, the year of the Penny Post, by Alderman T.J. Tomlinson as an iron and steel merchants in North Road; in 1884 the firm took over Durham goods station at Gilesgate for use as a warehouse. In 1910 John and George Archibald purchased the business and it was extended by incorporating departments for building materials and furniture. In 1924 William McIntyre, grandfather of the present managing director, bought out the Archibalds. Further expansion included the St Giles's parish hall, acquired in 1938, and a small shop on North Road, bought in 1942. In 1956 a purpose-built department store was built at the bottom of North Road and renamed Jagal (derived from the initial letters of J. and G. Archibald's Ltd) House; it was used until 1995. In 1996 there were plans to build a new DIY store on the Dragonville Industrial Estate. The City Baths also have a long history. Not all local comment has been favourable. Shortly after the Enabling Act, the City Baths were erected in 1855 and before the introduction of filtration the water's texture was described as treacly. In 1876 the City Council threatened to sell the Baths but a government enquiry saved them and they were renovated. The mayor in 1895 was Dr Jepson, an enthusiastic swimmer and supporter of the Amateur Swimming Club, which was founded in 1861. Partly because of the ASA's pressure new baths were erected in 1932; all the water was circulated, filtered, chlorinated and aerated once every four hours, and separate entrances provided for men and women. There has been an ice-rink in Durham since 1940, but there is no provision for one in the Walkergate Scheme currently being implemented. Yet Durham has long had a considerable reputation for skating: in 1895 Dr Jepson had organized 'Skating for the Unemployed' on the River Wear during a great freeze.

The photographs in this volume include some rare examples, such as the picture of the Worthy Brothers in about 1870. Shoe and boot makers from the Sands, they put on comedy acts to entertain customers in the Travellers' Rest at Claypath. Another shows the widening of Framwellgate Bridge in 1859. Others, depicting harvest time at Old Durham Farm in the 1890s and Shincliffe Mill in about 1900, remind us of the rural nature of Durham's immediate environment. The photograph of the Chains in Lower Gilesgate recalls one possible origin of the name: horses and carts were assisted up the steep Claypath Bank by chain horses.

The photograph of the Duke of Kent (the present Duke's father) visiting the Haig Homes on the Sherburn Road Estate in 1937 is a sad comment on the decline of our social awareness in the intervening period. The Duke inspected the homes thoroughly, commenting on the panoramic view from the rear towards Durham City and on the well-kept nature of the gardens. But sadly Sherburn Road has serious social problems in 1996, which it is hoped will be rectified by an imaginative scheme proposed for the area. The portrait of Thomas Brown by the well-known Durham photographer Daisy Edis commemorates an interesting character. Examples of his metalwork are to be found all over the city, especially in the Castle, Cathedral and University. He was both a locksmith and a blacksmith; for example he made the processional cross for St Giles's Church.

Durham has always aroused great loyalty from its citizens. The photograph of boys from the Bluecoat School at Claypath recalls the history of a school which was first established in 1708 and is now located at Newton Hall. Bishop Shute Barrington, who did so much for education in County Durham, bought the Claypath site in 1811. The Revd Andrew Bell was Master of Sherburn Hospital from 1809 and his 'Madras system' of monitorial teaching was used in the school for many years. William Goundry, the Master from 1821 to 1850, had been trained at the Barrington School in Bishop Auckland. The room for the boys measured only 36 ft by 28 ft, but numbers rose from 207 in 1826 to 391 in 1844 (there were 108 and 236 girls respectively) – the overcrowding must have been terrible but so much was Goundry's teaching admired that we are told by Carlton in his *History of Charities in the City of Durham* (1872), that 'the difficult task was sometimes assigned to him of developing the intellect of tradesmen's sons whose stupidity had caused all other Masters in the City to fail'.

William Noel Hodgson, the First World War poet educated at Durham School, wrote in one of his poems:

> And so we passed and others had our room,
> But well we know that here till days shall cease
> While the great stream goes seaward and trees bloom,
> God's kindness dwells about these courts of peace.

Professor G.R. Batho
Durham, 1996

SECTION ONE

MEET THE PEOPLE

Two Durham characters, c. 1870. Bill and Jim Worthy of the Sands were shoe and bootmakers. Well known as 'The Worthy Brothers', they were regular comedy entertainers at the Travellers' Rest beer-house at 72 Claypath. Both died in about 1890.

Robert Savage of 56 Hallgarth Street, shoe-maker and later cow-keeper, *c.* 1880. He was the author's great-great-grandfather. He died on 8 November 1894, five days after his wife, and is buried in St Oswald's cemetery, where a large four-sided granite column records generations of family deaths.

Margaret Savage, née Bone, Robert's wife, also photographed in about 1880. She died on 3 November 1894.

Three members of the Savage family of Gilesgate in their Sunday best, *c.* 1909. Left to right: James Edward Savage (the author's grandfather), Ambrose Savage and Frederick Thomas Savage (the author's great-grandfather). F.T. Savage was the son of Robert and Margaret (*see* page 8).

George Procter snr of 8 Market Place, publisher, printer and stationer, *c.* 1870. He came to Durham in about 1847 as a stationer and printer and acquired the business of the late Mr T. Hoggett. For many years Mr Procter was the Pant Master (*see* page 24).

George Henderson Procter jnr, JP, son of the above, carried on his father's business. He became a member of the city council in 1897, representing Neville's Cross ward. This photograph shows him after he was elected mayor in 1905. He lived at Flass House.

Ralph Salkeld of 173 Gilesgate (*see* page 40), photographed by John R. Edis in 1899. Born in 1846, Ralph attended the Model School when it was opened in 1858. After leaving school in 1860 he started work as an apprentice printer for the *Durham County Advertiser*. By 1873 he had become its managing director.

A garden party at The Laurels, Sherburn Road Ends, 28 August 1911. The deputy mayor, Councillor W.H. Wood, who owned the mineral water works in Gilesgate, was entertaining Lord and Lady Londonderry, then Mayor and Mayoress of Durham. Included in the party were the Countess of Ilchester, Viscountess Castlereagh, Lord Stewart, Lord Stavordale, Lady Mary Fox Strangeways, the Hon. Maureen Stewart, Captain Apperley and Mr Malcolm Dillon.

The Revd Westley Bothamley, *c.* 1920. He was vicar of St Nicholas's Church from 1904 to 1929, and was a familiar sight on the steps of the Londonderry statue in the Market Place, conducting open air services as part of his ministry.

William Appleby, cart-builder and hawker, with his wife Sarah, photographed at the Stable Yard, Sherburn Road Ends, in about 1910. Mr Appleby, who lived at 2 Maynards Row, Gilesgate, made milk-carts.

Mr J. Elliott of the Royal Ancient Order of Buffaloes (RAOB) in his regalia, *c.* 1920. Mr Elliott and his wife ran the Sun Inn at 34 Hallgarth Street (now a private house). He was also a prison warder.

Mrs Jane Herbert of Claypath, *c.* 1910. In September 1926, when Mrs Herbert died, the *Durham County Advertiser* described her as 'a hard-working industrious woman, a real friend to the sick and afflicted, and a generous helper of the Durham branch of the Salvation Army'.

Mr Ernest Bone and his daughter Louie, dressed up for the Whit Monday Parade, *c.* 1930. They were given a regular supply of bananas as a form of sponsorship for their advertising.

Mrs Margaret Ashworth (left), and her sister Lizzie Burnip outside 127 Gilesgate in the late 1920s. The children are James (left) and John. These small cottages, built in the 1840s on the site of older dwellings, overlook the Duck Pond (Gilesgate Green).

James and Elizabeth Dent outside their home, 129 Gilesgate, in the 1920s. Notice the old wooden shutters. Mr Dent ended his days as one of the brethren at Sherburn Hospital. In 1854 Joseph Burnell, tallow-chandler and pipe-maker, was listed as occupying 129/130, then one house.

The Sisterhood of the Gilesgate Methodist Church (founded 1912), photographed in 1932. Back row, starting fifth from the left, Mrs Edith Hewitt, Mrs Saville and Mrs Kelly; third row, right: Mrs Harker; second row, first, third, sixth, and seventh from the left, Mrs Middleton, Mrs Goodyear, Mrs Lightfoot and Mrs Wallace; front row, fourth and sixth from left, Mrs Haggis and Mrs Bush. The Methodist movement began in Gilesgate in August 1865 and meetings were held in a small room near the Toll Gate at the Road Ends.

Winifred French and her sister Margaret on the cannon, The Battery, Wharton Park, *c.* 1935. The Battery was built in 1858. The cannon was taken away and melted down for the war effort in August 1940. Under the barrel of the cannon can be seen the spire of St Nicholas's Church in the Market Place.

The Duke of York (later King George VI) visited Durham on 7 November 1929. From left to right: coroner John Graham (aged 96), wearing the uniform of the Sunderland Rifle Volunteers; the town clerk, Mr G.A. Carpenter; the recorder, Mr J.S.G. Pemberton; the mayor, Councillor W.W. Wilkinson; the Duke of York; Lord Londonderry. The Duke had stopped off at Durham on his way back to London after visiting Sunderland Bridge.

These men, wearing their Sunday best, were photographed outside Hallgarth Farm, Elvet, in the 1920s. The man with the beard is Mr Pattinson, father of Alderman John William Pattinson, owner of the Dunelm Hotel & Café, Old Elvet. The whippet was called Emma.

'Scottie on guard' outside Walton's café in Saddler Street in 1938. The café is now Whitegates' estate agents' office. The pram is the Rolls-Royce of its day, and sports chrome mudguards. The dog appears to be wearing false teeth!

The Duke of Kent visited the Haig Homes at Sutherland Place in Sherburn Road in July 1937. In this picture the Duke is conversing with Mr George Humpherson and his wife Edith. To the left of the Duke is Mr Thomas Parkin. The homes were purpose-built to house gravely disabled ex-soldiers and their families. While the Duke was there he admired the well-tended gardens and the panoramic view of the city from the rear of the property.

Bob Allan, scout leader, *c.* 1938. He was Rover leader of Pittington Rover Crew from 1930 to 1937 and then became leader of the Flambard Crew on its formation in the city in 1937. He was also secretary of the Raby Rover Crew; their leader was Lord Barnard, the County Commissioner. Bob started work at Sherburn Hill colliery and later went to Mackay's carpet factory, where he worked for thirty-eight years.

The wedding of Pilot Officer David Coates and Thelma Evans of Langley Moor at St Giles's Church on 6 September 1958. David Coates was the cub-master, and the guard of honour shows scouts and cubs of the 4th Durham (Gilesgate) troop. Mr Coates has enjoyed a lifelong association with St Giles's.

The mayor, Alderman G. McIntyre, walking across Elvet Bridge, 21 May 1952. He was the son of W. McIntyre (*see* page 72). To the right of the mayor is the town clerk, Martin Jones. Leading the procession is Jack Harrison, the mace bearer. Notice the granite sets which were once a feature of Durham streets.

William Willoughby, *c.* 1961. He worked as a gardener at Sandringham before coming to work at Wynyard Hall in the early 1900s. For many years he lived in Malvern Villas, Sherburn Road, and was gardener to three former mayors: W.H. Wood, F.W. Goodyear and W.W. Wilkinson.

Fr. Kenny, St Joseph's, Gilesgate Moor, 1948. Ordained at Kieran's College, County Kilkenny, his birthplace, he came to St Joseph's in 1948. He was a popular figure in Durham, always having time to talk to people of all denominations.

Thomas Ernest Brown, locksmith and blacksmith of Walkergate, photographed by Daisy Edis in about 1961. One of the city's oldest craftsmen, his steady hand and skill made him the champion safe-breaker in the city. There was no lock he could not pick, and the police used to call on his services if they were in any difficulty. A great deal of his wrought ironwork still survives in and around the city. One of his last creations was the processional cross at St Giles's Church. His business is still carried on today under the guidance of Peter Brown, his grandson, trading as T.E. Brown & Sons.

A visit to the Vane Tempest Hall (Gilesgate Community Centre) by Lord Londonderry, April 1952. Front, left to right: -?-, J.W. Simpson, -?-, Councillor Mrs P. Richardson, Lord Londonderry, W. McIntyre, Anne Simpson, Donald ('Danny') Webster.

JP Basil Sadler's retirement party in October 1948 was organized by colleagues associated with Durham County Hospital. The photograph includes John Corrigan, Alan Monro, Arthur Todd, Wilf Moss, Mr McDonald, Cuthbert Adamson, Knib Young, Hamilton Barclay, Basil Sadler, Frank Hare and Mr Bewick.

SECTION TWO

BUILT ENVIRONMENT

The Londonderry statue in the Market Place, 1870s. Sculpted by Raffaelle Monti, the statue was unveiled on 2 December 1861 in the presence of Benjamin Disraeli. The statue was commissioned by Frances Anne, Lady Londonderry, at a cost of £2,000 paid in advance. Before the statue was delivered Monti went bankrupt, and the sculpture was seized by his creditors; Lady Londonderry had to pay a further £1,000 before it was handed over. The base was erected by a local mason, Mr T. Winter. The shop to the left of the statue is Birkenshaw's, bootmakers, now the Tourist Information Office.

Framwellgate Bridge, *c.* 1859. On 6 July 1859 a motion was passed by the Local Board of Health to widen and improve the bridge. The shop on the left was that of Bowey, confectioners.

Market day in the Market Place, *c.* 1870. Neptune is on his second pant, which was designed by E.R. Robson in September 1863. All that remains of the site now is a small octagon of granite sets (*see* page 35).

The view from Mountjoy, *c.* 1870. The field to the left is now St Oswald's cemetery, in the centre is School House and on the right Oswald Court Council Flats. The lane still continues along the same route, linking up to Church Street.

St Oswald's Church, *c.* 1880. It is believed that a church occupied the present site before the Norman Conquest. Around the end of the twelfth century the present church was virtually rebuilt. One famous Victorian incumbent was the Revd Dr John Bacchus Dykes who was vicar from 1862 to 1876. He composed many fine hymn tunes. His memorial stands in the old cemetery opposite the church, now a children's playing area.

St Margaret's Church, Crossgate, *c.* 1920. The church dates from the middle of the twelfth century. Below the churchyard wall can be seen one of the city fire-ladders. This area is now an open car park.

Elvet Methodist Church, Old Elvet, *c.* 1903. The foundation stone was laid on 23 July 1902 by the Earl of Durham and the official opening took place on 4 November 1903. The architect was Mr Morley of Bradford. The total cost of the church was about £10,000 and at the time of the opening over £6,000 of this had been collected. (*See also* page 114.)

St Cuthbert's Roman Catholic Church, Old Elvet, *c.* 1950. Designed and built by Ignatius Bonomi, it was opened on 31 May 1827. The tower was added to the west end in 1869.

Gilesgate Methodist Church, 1991. The chapel was opened for divine worship on Monday 8 January 1869. The cost of the building was about £600, and Mr James Willan gave £250 towards it. In 1912 the property behind the chapel was purchased for £150. The photograph was taken shortly before the chapel closed in 1992, a great loss to Gilesgate. It now awaits development, possibly into student accommodation.

The chancel of St Giles's Church, *c.* 1927. On the far right is the wooden effigy of John Heath of Kepier (d. 1590), patron of the church.

St Giles's Church, *c.* 1883. The old headstones were removed in 1964. Out of almost 300 only 38 were saved, the rest being discarded as of no artistic or historical interest!

Bethel Chapel (Methodist New Connection), North Road, *c.* 1953. The foundation stone was laid on 4 May 1853 and it was opened on 13 August 1854. It was built in the Roman Ionic style at an estimated cost of £3,000 by E.R. Robson, to the design of his seventeen-year-old son. Robson of Durham later became known for his designs for elementary schools and municipal buildings throughout the country.

Neville's Cross College, *c.* 1921. The College was begun in June 1913 but because of the First World War it was not completed until 1921. It is now the Neville's Cross Centre of New College, Durham.

Chambers' Yard, Claypath, *c.* 1920. Named after Councillor James Chambers, a local prominent Wesleyan Methodist, it was situated to the rear of 27 Claypath. It is now the site of the old Palladium cinema, which was opened 18 March 1929.

The Tower, Neville's Cross, 1890s. This was the home of Mr J. Forster, an architect and builder. In the 1870s he bought land in the Neville's Cross area which was developed as The Avenue. The Tower is now a private nursing home called Farnley Tower.

Hillcrest House, Potter's Bank, Elvet Moor, *c.* 1908. This was the residence of Mr M. Dean.

Springwell Hall, the home of Colonel W.H. Ritson, *c.* 1908. It was built in the 1860s by Joseph Love, a colliery owner, and at that time it was called Mount Beulah. In 1936 the building was converted into St Leonard's Roman Catholic Secondary Modern School.

The view from the bottom of Walkergate in the 1870s. The cottage on the right of the arch was demolished shortly after this photograph was taken and replaced by a dye-house for Henderson's carpet factory. In 1909 this in turn was converted into the Palace Theatre. The wall on the left is the retaining wall for the Durham Indoor Markets.

This is the yard visible through the arch in the top photograph in about 1870. Bailes the printers operated from here for many years. This area was cleared in the early 1960s to make way for the new Millburngate Bridge.

Looking up Walkergate (or Palace Lane) towards Claypath, 1930s. Walkergate was named after the trade, 'walker' meaning fuller or cloth-worker. In December 1909 a roller-skating rink was opened in Walkergate by the mayor, W.H. Wood. The building at the top right is St Nicholas's Church Hall.

The Palace Theatre, Walkergate, February 1964. It was opened on 9 August 1909 by Mr T.C. Rawes. A mixture of music-hall acts and films was presented, and famous performers included Charlie Chaplin and Jimmy James. Many old maps and documents refer to this area as Back Lane. The poster on the right is advertising the last film to be screened at the Palace.

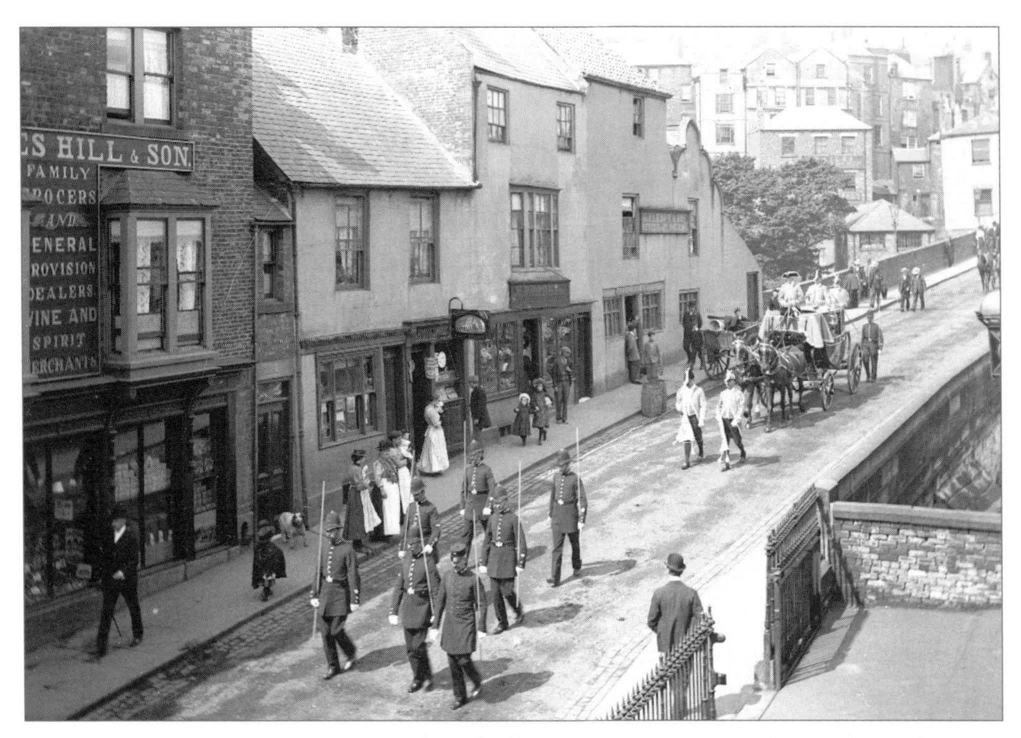

Policemen in ceremonial dress escorting the judges' procession passing over Elvet Bridge to the Assize Courts, *c*. 1900. Front row: PCs Scott and Anderson, Inspector Harnby; second row: PCs Lay and Fowler; third row: Sgt Thompson, PC Roberts; behind the coach is PC Atkinson.

Durham Market Place, August 1901. Construction of the men's underground toilets is in progress. The *Durham County Advertiser* reported on the new toilets in detail, describing the marble mosaic floor and walls, and the ivory white and green-glazed brick ceiling. There were six urinals and also two water-closets, each provided with a penny-in-the-slot lock. These toilets were removed in the early 1970s when the Market Place was pedestrianized and repaved.

The removal of Neptune from the Market Place in 1923 marked the end of about five hundred years of continuous public water supply to the centre of the city. This had begun in 1450 when Thomas Billingham granted the spring at Fram Well for the use of the city. This, the third of the pants, was erected in 1902. Money for it was given by Miss Ellen Gibson.

Durham baths and wash-house, *c.* 1900. The first baths were built in 1855 at a cost of £5,000. The Corporation fire-engine was also housed there. The new baths, costing just over £31,000, were opened in 1932 by Lord Barnard.

Two views looking down Millburngate from the bottom of Framwellgate. The top photograph was taken in about the early 1900s, and the bottom photograph in the 1930s. This area is now part of Millburngate shopping centre.

A bird's-eye view from the cathedral tower looking over Millburngate and Framwellgate, *c.* 1964. In the distance is the newly built County Hall. This was at one time a highly populated area which, in later years, became mainly slum dwellings.

New Elvet in the late 1920s. Small retail shops now occupy this site, opposite Dunelm House. This street scene is typical of the slum housing conditions in Durham at the time.

Church Lane, looking towards St Oswald's vicarage, in 1938. The lane still exists and links Hallgarth Street to Church Street.

Looking towards Durham from Sherburn Road Ends, *c.* 1900. The large house with the bow windows, on the left, is The Mount, which occupied the site of the old Toll House. On the right is Gilesgate Methodist Chapel (*see* page 27).

The newly planted avenue of trees at the top of Gilesgate, 1890s. On the left is the site of the ancient duck pond, removed in 1850. St Giles's Church records show that in 1595 new stocks were made, which stood on the Green.

Looking up Gilesgate Bank, *c.* 1930. The steepness of Gilesgate Bank has created many problems over the years. On 12 May 1882 a horse drawing a rolley from the North Eastern Railway Company, transporting a load of bark to Mr Summer's tanyard, dropped down dead at the summit of the bank. The horse had appeared in perfect health just before the approach.

Salkeld's chimney at 173 Gilesgate, at the bottom of Gilesgate Bank, *c.* 1963. Its unusual flying buttress design only came to light as the surrounding property was being demolished. The chimney was taken down.

Moody's Buildings, which stood between Gilesgate roundabout and the Woodman Inn, *c.* 1965. They were demolished to make way for the new through road in the 1960s.

Lower Gilesgate, 1920s. The old Woodman Inn is on the right. Lower Gilesgate was originally the main route into the city before Leazes Road was opened in the late 1960s. The pile of granite sets on the left is a reminder of Durham's constant battle to maintain its over-used roads.

The Chains in Lower Gilesgate, photographed from Claypath in about 1900. The property on the left was a tenement dwelling known as Jacob's Ladder and the shop was McCartan's. The Chains council flats were built on the site in the late 1940s. The name is believed to derive from the days when chain horses used to help horse and carts up Claypath Bank.

The view up Claypath, *c.* 1910. The spire in the centre is that of the United Reform Church. This is still the only road into Durham which does not cross a river.

SECTION THREE

SCHOOLDAYS & SPORT

The former Johnston Grammar Technical School in South Street (now demolished), seen from St Margaret's churchyard, c. 1962. The school's foundation was made possible by a bequest of £3,200 by James Finlay Weir Johnston (1796–1855). Durham County Council gave £2,000. The school was built by Messrs Gradon & Sons of North Road, to a design by Messrs Oliver & Leeson of Newcastle. The school moved to the Crossgate site in 1954.

Theatrical performers at the Johnston School, *c.* 1917. The first headmaster, Mr S. Whalley, is on the far right. The foundation stone was laid by the Earl of Durham on 2 August 1899, and the school officially opened on 23 June 1901.

Durham School fire engine, photographed by John Edis in about 1906. Durham School is one of the oldest in England and can trace its origins back to medieval times. In 1844 the school moved from Palace Green to the present site, which was originally Bellasis House.

A class from St Margaret's school, Margery Lane, Crossgate, 1912. Back row, left to right: Wright, -?-, Bob Allan, Robinson, Tulip, Dodds, Taylor, Spirit. Third row: Culbert, Watts, Wright, Cullingford, Hopper, Shawcross, Wise, Pollard. Second row: Liddle, Snowball, Hall, Mr A.V. Yockney (headmaster), Smith, -?-, Hall. Front row: Cooper, Trotter, Morgan, Wilson, Bowen, Fairless.

A performance at St Margaret's school, *c.* 1911. The school was built on land which was formerly known as West Orchard and opened in January 1861. The school yard has recently been used for a small housing development consisting of flats to let.

Bluecoat boys in fancy dress, *c.* 1911.

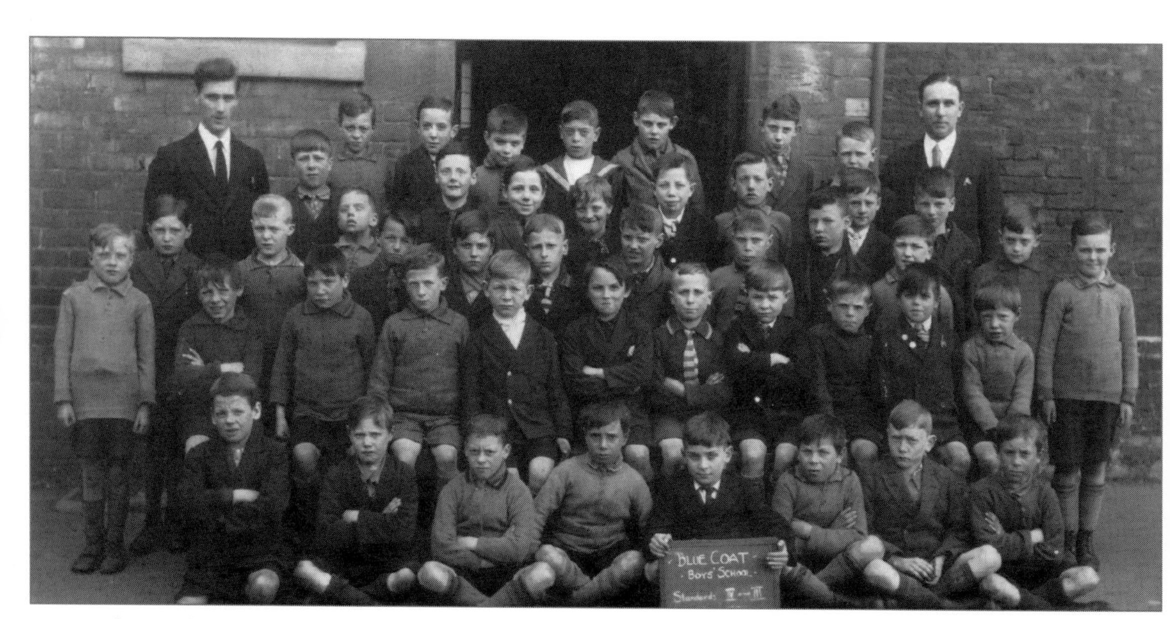

Bluecoat boys, Claypath, May 1931. The school dates back to 1708 when it had only six boys; they were joined in 1736 by six girls. The school moved to the Claypath site in 1811.

Mrs Porter's private school at 1 Princes Street, Western Hill, *c.* 1934. Mrs Porter is fifth from the left in the centre row. The young lady third from the left in the centre row later became Mrs Margaret Oliver, wife of John Oliver, fishmonger of Millburngate.

Durham City schoolchildren in the Market Place preparing to take part in the King George VI coronation celebrations, May 1937. Three thousand children marched from the Market Place to the cathedral, led by the Shakespeare Band (*see* page 94). They were welcomed by the Dean of Durham, Dr Cyril Alington. Sports events were held on the city cricket ground in the afternoon.

Baths Bridge on Regatta day, *c.* 1920. The bridge, with its steel lattice design, was erected in 1894. The present concrete construction replaced it in June 1962.

Durham City Amateur Swimming Club, *c.* 1910. This picture shows the old baths which were built in the 1850s. The water was said to be a peaty brown colour because of the lack of filtration. The club was founded in 1861.

Durham City Amateur Swimming Club, 1933. High board, left to right: Johnny Heckles, Ken Spirit, Geoff Howe. Middle board: Bill Watson, Ted Storey, Harry Bell, Vic Dobson, Norman Sarsfield, Cud Lax. Bottom: Frank Archer, Joe Higgins, George Saynor, Tom Rickerby, Frank Webster, A.P. Dobson, Jimmy Smurthwaite, Bill McIntyre. The new baths were opened in 1932.

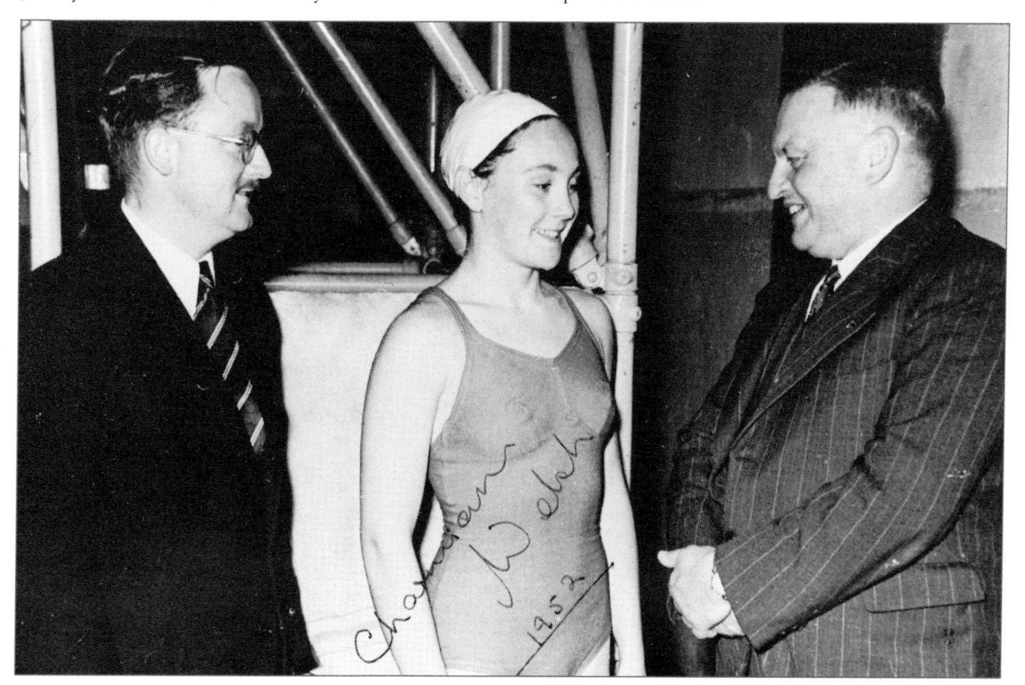

A presentation by Alderman Ferens of a 3 metre springboard to the city baths, 1952. Left to right: Norman Sarsfield, Charmian Welsh and Cecil Ferens. Charmian was placed 5th in the springboard event at the 1952 Olympic Games in Helsinki.

St Leonard's RC School swimming team, *c.* 1948. Left to right: F. Walters, P. Bond, H. Thompson, W. Howie, J. Moran.

Durham City Amateur Rowing Club, 1928. The club was established in 1860 and the new club-house is situated on the corner of the Racecourse opposite Old Durham Gardens.

Durham City Amateur Rowing Club, photographed after the first post-war regatta, June 1946. A regular annual event, the Durham Regatta dates back to 1834, when the university was established, and is believed to be one of the oldest in the country.

St Cuthbert's Mission football team, Framwellgate Moor, 1909. The Mission was attached to St Cuthbert's Church in North Road.

Elvet Wanderers football team, 1908. Most parishes in the city had their own football teams.

St Margaret's rugby football team, 1911. The teachers were Mr Reid (left) and Mr Yockney.

Bluecoat rugby football team, 1913. Many of their sporting trophies still exist at the new school at Newton Hall.

Neville's Cross Amateur Football Club, 1923.

Durham St Giles's football team, April 1948. Left to right: B. Lishman, Sid Hewitt, T. Flowers, ? Musgrove, A. Lockey, L. Tempest, B. Brunskill, R. Clark, W. Barker, T. Bunce, D. Tenwick, R. Dixon, Walter Forster.

Durham St Giles's football supporters, April 1948. Left to right: Joe Parkin, B. Simpson, T. Heath, E. Davey, J. Curry, K. Peacock (with glasses), H. Sands, T. Gavaghan, G. Cairns, J. Rowell, D. Adair.

Durham City football club's first match at Ferens Park, October 1951. Farmer Bill Hopps (seated on the left in the front row) of Old Durham farm (*see* page 80) provided the turf for the playing area and kicked off the first game against Sunderland A; unfortunately Durham lost 3–2. Cecil Ferens is in the centre of the front row (*see* page 96).

Vane Tempest judo club, Gilesgate, 1950s. Second from the left in the centre row is Tommy Rowntree, who for many years has been the postman at Durham University.

Alington House football team, *c.* 1952. Back row, left to right: H. McGregor, A. Forrester, G. Watson, P. Driver, E. Nicholson, B. Gibb, B. Barrass, F. Crago. Front row: S. Winter, K. Crampton, J. Snowdon, H. Troughear, F. Smithson.

SECTION FOUR

WORKING LIFE

The premises of Waites, farrier and general smith, and Joplings, undertakers and builders, at 26 Crossgate, 1900. On the left is Jonathan Waite. No. 26 Crossgate is now a private house and stands opposite the former St Margaret's Hospital.

Ramsbottom's pork butchers, 19 Silver Street, 1920s. For many years this was Dunn & Co., gentlemen's outfitters. To the right are the steps leading down to the riverbank footpath and the fulling mill.

The Brewer's Arms, 82 Gilesgate, 1870s. The property on the left was that of Arthur Thwaites, grocer. This was later taken over as the Brewer's Arms. Mr George Fowler (brother of Alderman James Fowler) started business in Gilesgate and became a tenant of the brewery. Mr Fowler lived at Eden Cottage, Gilesgate Moor.

Sarsfield's chemist shop, 7 Market Place, *c.* 1890. It was demolished in 1923 to make way for an extension to J. Backhouse & Co.'s bank. Above the shop can be seen the sign of the Bowes Arms Hotel. The business was originally founded in Saddler Street by Messrs Trueman and Thompson, and moved to the Market Place in about 1850. Mr Sarsfield took over the business in 1865.

Procter's printing and stationery shop (*see* page 10), 8 Market Place, *c.* 1920. Now the City Sports shop, it was previously the Evening Chronicle Offices.

Lockey's Supply Store & Café, 76 Saddler Street, 1920s. The firm was awarded a Gold Medal for tea blending, London 1907, and the Silver Medal, London 1908. The premises are now occupied by the Northern Rock Building Society.

E.T. Guire's, confectioner, at 56 Saddler Street, alongside Pullar's of Perth, dyers and cleaners, at no. 57, *c.* 1939.

Rushworth's Art Gallery, 61 Saddler Street, 1890s. This was originally the site of a Georgian Theatre, destroyed by fire in 1869. Many will remember the building as Sutton's sale-rooms. The site was cleared in the 1970s for student accommodation.

Tommy Martin (left) and Andrew Dimambro outside Dimambro's confectioner's and ice-cream shop, Elvet Bridge, *c.* 1930. They also had a business at 90 Claypath. Their ice-cream was famous throughout the city.

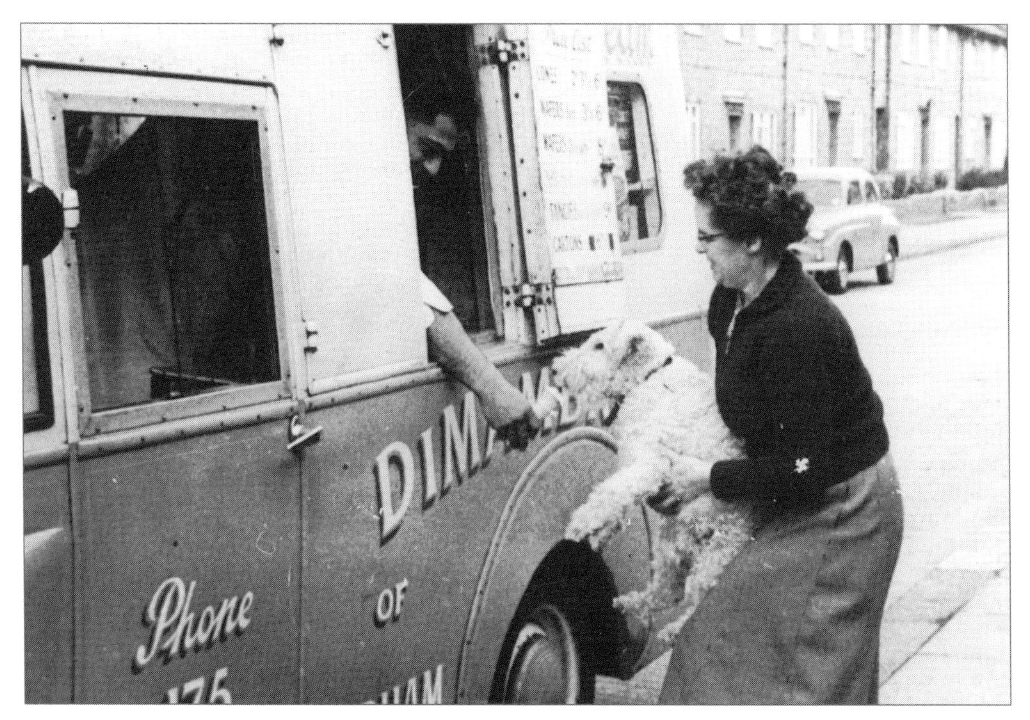

Dominic Dimambro with his ice-cream van in Annand Road, Gilesgate, in the 1950s. In those days you could afford to buy your dog an ice-cream!

Staff of the Claypath Co-operative Store pose for a coronation photograph in 1953. In the centre of the front row is Nicol Watson, and to his right is Gladys Ashworth. The shop was demolished in the 1960s to make way for the Claypath underpass development.

Gilesgate Co-op, 1 Sunderland Road, *c.* 1967. This was part of Annfield Plain Branch. This area was always known locally as the Store Corner. The buildings were demolished in the late 1960s to make way for a new shopping development, and the Motorist Discount Store now occupies the site at the Road Ends.

The Dunelm window cleaners attending to Hepworth's shop windows, Saddler Street, 6 September 1918. Left to right: Mrs R. Marshall, -?-, Miss W. Burke, Mr H.G. Marshall. The photograph was taken by Mr Stafford for the Speedy Photo Company, Durham.

John Oliver's fish and poultry shop, 2 North Road, 1920s. This was the oldest-established wet fish shop in the city, buying fresh fish from North Shields and Hartlepool daily. Later the Army & Navy Stores took over the premises. More recently it became Greenwell's delicatessen. It has since been demolished for redevelopment.

Waggott's tobacconists shop, 1 Bluecoat Buildings, Claypath, *c.* 1925. The gate on the left was one entrance to Bluecoat School. The shop is now occupied by an estate agent.

Woolworth's store, 17 Market Place, *c.* 1928. The property was previously the Rose and Crown Hotel, which at one time was owned by Sir John Duck, Durham's Dick Whittington. In 1710 it passed into the hands of the Tempest family. Woolworth's later had a new store built on the site.

North Road in the 1950s. The Essoldo Cinema, previously the Regal, was built by Gradon & Sons of North Road and was opened in March 1934 by the mayor, James C. Fowler. The building in the centre is the old Miners' Hall, and on the far right is the old Neville Hotel.

J. Tuke & Son, music and musical instrument dealers, 71 North Road, 1938.

The laying of the foundation stone for the extension to the Durham County Hospital, 7 May 1937, by the Marquis of Londonderry KG, MVO, and the Right Revd the Lord Bishop of Durham. The architects were Messrs Cordingley & McIntyre and the building contractors were Messrs George Gradon & Son.

Durham County permanent police staff, photographed by A.G. Humphrys in the 1920s. The City police force was amalgamated with the County force on 1 April 1921. The old City silver buttons were melted down and made into a crucifix for St Oswald's Church.

Staff at Blagdon's leather works, 114 Framwellgate, *c.* 1913. Second from the left is Mr Ernest Young of 3 Kepier Terrace, Gilesgate. The leather works closed in 1967 and the property was one of the last to be demolished in the lower Framwellgate area.

The workforce of George Gradon & Son, builders and timber merchants, North Road, *c.* 1932. Gradons erected many fine buildings in and around the city; the old Miners' Hall in North Road is an example. (*See* page 66.)

Miners from the Grange Colliery, Carrville, 1947. Left to right: D. Crawford, J. Bagnall, Billy Nichol, G. Barker, J. Clough, M. Hinds, W. Scott, A. Coyle, J. Gowland, ? Hamilton. The coal was mined from drifts in the woods and was originally hauled out through the woods by cable. As the drifts became deeper, the coal was brought to the surface by the old Grange Colliery shaft which had been broken into from one of the coal-drifts.

Mr Jack Reid, cobbler, of 111a Gilesgate, 1940s. Mr Reid started business in 1939, doing a great deal of work for the army. He retired in 1960.

The Bay Horse public house, 110 Gilesgate, showing Reid the cobbler's on the right, 1961. The public house is still trading but is now the Durham Light Infantryman and incorporates the shop.

Stanton's, at 128 Millburngate, Durham's most famous fried fish and chip shop, 1960s The shop was run by the Stanton brothers, John William and James Leon. Their grandfather founded the business with a shop in the Market Place. In the 1970s the business was bought by Bimbi's.

Williamson's butcher's shop, Crossgate Peth, 1960s. Above the front door is the name Clover Cottage. This property was demolished in the 1960s and a flower bed now occupies the site.

Mr William McIntyre, *c.* 1940. William bought out of Archibald's in 1924 and was the grandfather of the present managing director, Ian McIntyre. The business began in 1840 when Alderman T.J. Tomlinson opened his iron and steel business in North Road. Since those early days the business has grown to become a household name in the North-East.

Archibald's first shop at 9 North Road, 1951. Opened in 1942 by William McIntyre, it had previously been Leatham's ironmonger and gunsmith's shop.

The official opening of Jagal House, Archibald's new store in North Road, 29 February 1956. The Mayor, Councillor H.L. Cawood, JP, is cutting the ribbon, watched by Gordon McIntyre (right), and his wife and their son Ian (left).

Jagal House, North Road, 1962. The building was designed by Messrs Cordingley & McIntyre, and built by Messrs Holst & Co. Ltd. The store has recently been demolished for redevelopment.

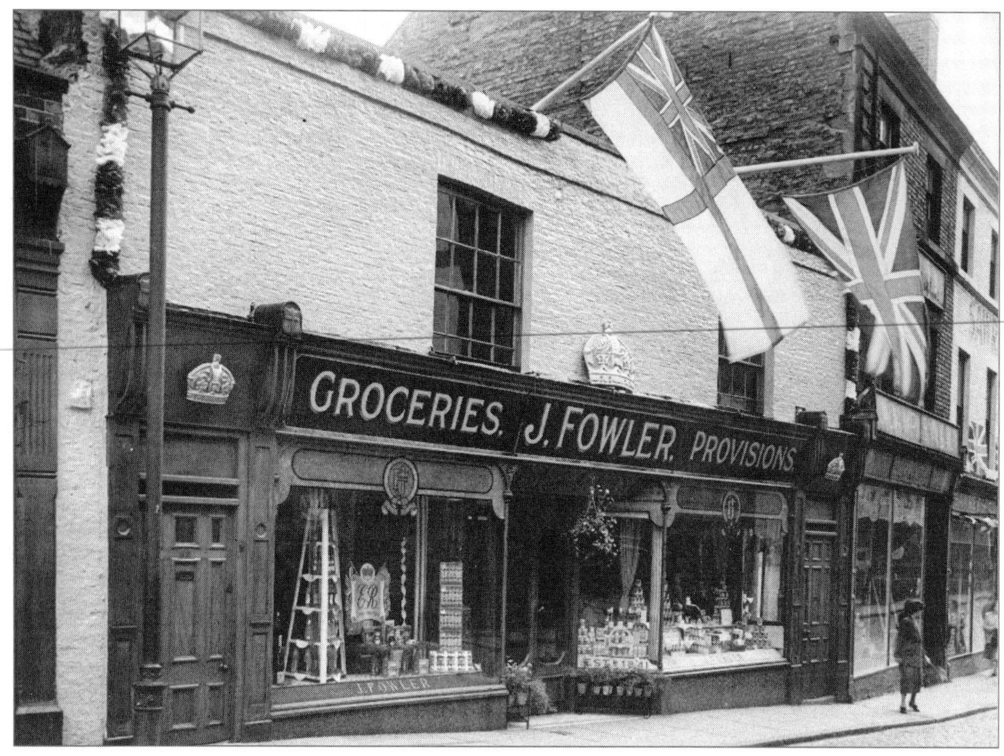

Fowler's grocer's shop, 99/100 Claypath, decorated for the coronation of Queen Elizabeth in 1953. The property was demolished in about 1970 to make way for the Claypath underpass.

The interior of Fowler's shop, 1953.

The view up North Road, opposite the bus station, in the late 1950s. Most of the property on the right was demolished and redeveloped in about 1970. On the far left is the Globe cinema, now an amusement arcade.

Staff of Durham Tax Office, photographed on the roof of Doggart's Department Store in about 1952. The tax office occupied the top floor. The premises are now occupied by Boot's the Chemists. Bluecoat school, Claypath, can be seen on the left in the background.

Tanker factory staff of Darham Industries (London) Ltd, Dragonville, June 1949.

The interior of Darham's tanker factory at Dragonville in the 1950s. The building is now occupied by Archibald's DIY store.

Joe Sanders weaving a carpet at Mackay's carpet factory, July 1960. This carpet was a gift from the citizens of Durham City to Princess Margaret on her wedding to Anthony Armstrong-Jones (Lord Snowdon).

Mr Stockwell making a presentation to Tommy Rowntree for making the most sales in a Chandy competition at Wood & Watson's pop factory, Gilesgate, 1961. Left to right: Pat Wheatley, Walter Watson, Steve Wilkinson, Jacky Chapelow, Brian Terry, John Wilson, Steve Hickman, Sam Westhead, Tony Naisbett, Ronnie Barker, Freddie Saville, Frank Fowler, Luke Peverall, Jack Andrews, Billy Bennett, Tommy Rowntree, Harold Thomas, Harry Wood, Mr Stockwell (the Chandy rep).

Constructing Bede chapel, *c.* 1939. The foundation stone was laid on 28 January 1939 by the Bishop of Durham, the Right Revd Herbert Hensley Henson DD. The architects were John Seely & Paul Paget of London. The contractors were Messrs John Jackson & Sons, Newcastle, and the total cost of the chapel was £11,000.

Slating Bede chapel roof, August 1939. The work was carried out by J. Hewitson of Newcastle upon Tyne and 17 tons of Westmorland slates were used.

The statue of Bede being erected at the front of the chapel, July 1939. Sculptured by E.J. Doudney, London, it weighed approximately a ton.

The cross being placed in position on Bede chapel roof, July 1939. The chapel doorway came from 103 Framwellgate, where the first students had lived in 1841.

The Hopps family of Old Durham farm, Old Durham gardens, 1890s. The bearded man in the centre is Richard Henry Hopps (born 1839); his wife, Penelope Jane, is to his left.

Old Durham farmhouse, *c.* 1908. It is now a private house.

Harvest time at Old Durham farm, 1890s. This is a fine example of rural life, as it captures everyone at work. The old barn on the left is now derelict and is to be converted into a private house.

The horse-gin at Old Durham farm, *c.* 1920. The name 'gin' is short for engine. These horse-powered gins were used to operate threshing machines. A great number were demolished when farm machinery developed and it is rare now to find a gin-house intact.

An aerial view of Bent House farm, Bent House Lane, *c.* 1954. The original farmhouse stands to the left of the present one, which is seen on the right.

Annie Isobella Hopps (née Laurie), wife of Richard Henry Hopps (born 1878), outside Bent House farm, *c.* 1909.

Mountjoy farm, *c.* 1950. This building is now a private house and most of the land has now been built on by the university. A small section of the original land is still farmed by the Stephenson family from Bearpark.

Bob Stephenson (left) and Clive Routledge ploughing with a team of horses on Mountjoy farm, *c.* 1938.

Shincliffe Mill, *c.* 1890. The earliest reference to the mill was in 1303 and in 1598 an indictment was issued for the murder of Margaret Noble at Shincliffe Mill. From 1861 to 1889 the mill was worked by Stephen Oliver, who had taken over from his father. It was demolished in about 1900 and the Old Durham Fever Hospital was built on the site in 1911 for forty patients. It is now Shincliffe Kennels.

Hallgarth tithe barn, Elvet, *c.* 1880. The barn was originally used as a granary for Durham Priory in the fifteenth century. It now serves as the Durham prison officers' club.

SECTION FIVE

LEISURE

The Cock Inn, New Elvet, 1880s. This building was demolished in the 1960s, and the site is now the entrance to the Three Tuns car-park. Notice the blocked-in window of the property on the left. This was probably done to evade window tax, which was first introduced in 1697. This is a good example of a typical eighteenth-century Durham house.

Harry Wilby, with his son Walter in the doorway of the Lambton Arms, 101 Framwellgate, *c.* 1910. The pub was known locally as 'the Painted House' because of the well-kept appearance of the paint work, which was maintained by the brewery.

The old Neville's Cross working men's club, in the late 1920s. This cottage was previously known as Colpitts' Cottage after the Colpitts family, wine and spirit merchants. On the right is Thomas Reed, the club steward. The tall chimney on the left belonged to the Neville's Cross laundry.

A ladies' outing from the Neville Hotel, 18 North Road, in the late 1940s. This photograph was taken at the bottom of Neville Street (*see* page 66).

The old yard-of-ale glass in use in the Victoria public house, 86 Hallgarth Street, 1960s. Second from the right at the back is Arthur Wilby, the chimney sweep (*see* page 111).

Skating on the Wear, February 1895. The mayor, Dr Jepson, arranged 'Skating for the Unemployed', during the great freeze when temperatures dropped well below zero. Dr Jepson worked with the tradespeople and city folk to organize races on the river, and prizes of groceries and provisions were given. The races were run from the Museum Stakes (by the Fulling Mill) to Framwellgate Bridge.

A re-enactment of the past at Kepier Gatehouse showing one of the brethren handing over salmon, caught from the Wear, to the master of the hospital, *c.* 1900.

Gilesgate Cousins, photographed at the rear of the Smiths' Arms, 103 Gilesgate, 1892. The Cousins were a vegetable and flower society. Their rivals were the Gilligate Giants, a similar group.

Durham City Field and Research Club at Finchale Abbey, 1901. Third from the right in the back row is Ralph Salkeld (*see* page 11). The club held its meetings in the Burlison Art Gallery in the Town Hall. In the winter months they were entertained by various speakers showing lantern slides of local scenes and wildlife.

Committee members of the Durham City Horse Parade, standing outside the Barracks, Vane Tempest Hall, *c.* 1927. The committee held its meetings in various Durham hotels; whist drives and dances were organized to raise funds for expenses and prizes. The first parade took place in 1903 and, after a gap of seven years, it was revived in 1910. The parades were held to raise funds for the Durham County Hospital. In the centre of the middle row is Sydney Wood; in the front row in the dark jacket is Mr W. Tindale; to the far right is Mr T. Pawson.

Wood & Watson's entry in the Durham City Horse Parade, *c.* 1920. The two gentlemen in suits in the centre are Bill and Sydney Wood, sons of the founder, W.H. Wood, owner of the Aerated Water Works. In later years classes were introduced for motor vehicles (1927) and jazz bands (1928). The parade died out in the late 1930s.

Fentimans' entry for the Horse Parade, *c.* 1910. Fentimans, the botanical brewers, were based at Prospect Works, Hallgarth Street. Fentimans' Direct Supply ceased to trade in the early 1970s.

Fowler's cart from Claypath, decorated to advertise their China tea, *c.* 1925. The man holding the horse is Jack Pickering from Palace Lane. The photograph was taken outside 134–135 Gilesgate.

The New Street Gang, *c.* 1926. Back row, left to right: Jimmy Goldsborough, -?-, ? Rought, Ken Spirit, Doug Kiddie. Front row: Eric Clarkson, Jimmy Lee, Andrew Richie. New Street stands behind the present bus station in North Road.

Members of Claypath YMCA, 85 Claypath, *c.* 1938. Meetings were held above Benny Clark's cycle shop. Left to right: Gordon McGowan, Tommy Grimes, -?-, -?-, -?-, Billy Hall, Amy Appleby, Tommy Simpson, Fred Cleckner, Ken Cleckner. The man holding the case and the two men on the right are unknown.

Durham City Gypsy Juvenile jazz band, 1931. Left to right: Nora Scruby, Mary Wager, Tommy Wager. The Gypsy Juveniles were founded in the 1920s by Mr Barton in the Framwellgate and Millburngate areas of the City.

St Oswald's choir, *c.* 1920. Frank Eves is fifth from the left. The processional cross, which dates from Tudor times, was discovered in a portmanteau left in a mail coach in a Durham hotel yard in the middle of the nineteenth century. It was given to the then incumbent, Dr Dykes, for the church.

Durham Shakespeare Temperance Band at the Rink, Wharton Park, *c.* 1936. In November 1936 the band took part in the civic service procession to Durham Cathedral, led by the newly elected mayor, Lord Londonderry and his guest, the German Ambassador, Joachim von Ribbentrop.

Gilesgate jazz band, standing on the 'Duff Heap', Sunderland Road, *c.* 1933.

Durham Miners' Gala, *c.* 1948. Here the crowds are walking over Elvet Bridge for the service at Durham Cathedral.

The mayor, Alderman Cecil Ferens, being rowed down the river by Sea Rangers from Durham High School and St Oswald's school, after officially launching the boat in October 1948.

Members of Sherburn Road Youth Club, on the Sherburn Road Estate, performing one of Al Jolson's musicals in the early 1950s. The man in the bowler hat on the left is Ken Peacock, who ran the wet fish shop in Saddler Street.

Durham ice rink, *c*. 1947. On 8 March 1940 the canvas-topped rink was opened to the public for the first time. After a fire in the early 1940s, the rink was rebuilt and re-opened in 1947.

The Christie organ and organist at the Regal Cinema, 8 North Road, *c*. 1938. The Regal later became the Essoldo.

Durham City Corporation wagon, *c.* 1927. This was an entrant for the Whit Monday Parade, photographed outside 133–134 Gilesgate. Note the solid tyres.

Bill Longstaff, a coal-miner from Sherburn Village, with one of his engines at the model engineers' club at the Vane Tempest Hall, April 1951. The Queen's Head public house car park is in the background.

Members of the Durham City Photographic Society at their annual dinner in the Shakespeare Hall, North Road, 1957. Daisy Edis is seated in the centre. The society was founded in 1892 by the Revd G.T. Fox, vicar of St Nicholas's Church.

Canon C.J. Thurlow presenting a trophy to St Margaret's Billiards/Snooker Club, St Margaret's Church hall, Crossgate, April 1952. Twice champion at the Club in the 1930s, he is showing members that he was still capable of winning the trophy himself.

Gilesgate Welfare Fur Society (Vane Tempest Hall), February 1952. Front row, left to right: Danny Bates, Jim Scott, Jack Iley, William McIntyre (president), Les Dent, George Aither. Rabbit breeding became very popular during the Second World War, as meat was rationed and any fresh meat was highly prized.

Mayoress Evelyn Blyth leaving the rear of the County Hotel with dignitaries from the Durham Miners' Gala, 1954. Front row, left to right: Bessie Braddock, Sam Watson, -?-, Aneurin Bevan, Mrs Blyth, -?-, -?-, -?-.

SECTION SIX

TRANSPORT

An advertisement for Cowie's motor cycles, Earls Court, Gilesgate, 1958. The building was originally St Giles's parish hall but it was taken over by Archibald's as Jagal House in 1938. It was demolished in the late 1960s to make room for the Gilesgate roundabout.

A Northern General Transport bus in Durham Market Place, in the late 1920s. The bus is a 1920 Daimler, taken over in 1924 from Isaac Walton's Crescent Bus Company of Gateshead who built the body. Conductresses had been employed during the First World War and they were retained as the firm expanded. This bus was in direct competition with the Sunderland District bus pictured below.

Sunderland & District Tramways bus in Durham Market Place, *c.* 1925. No. 56 was an AEC 2-tonner with coachwork by United at their Lowestoft factory. The Sunderland District Omnibus Co. Ltd was formed in 1927. This competed with, and was taken over by, Northern in 1931.

A 1948 Leyland Tiger from the Express Omnibus Co. (owned by the Showler family), Gilesgate Moor. The front of the bus reads 'Sherburn Hospital'. The Express Co. later became amalgamated into Durham District Services.

A Gillett & Baker bus crossing over Framwellgate Bridge in 1946. This bus ran to Waddington Street where it turned round for the G&B West Hartlepool service. Gilletts sold the business to United in 1974.

The police box in Durham Market Place in 1958, photographed shortly after the television monitors were installed. Two cameras were mounted on tall poles, one at the bottom of Silver Street to monitor traffic on Framwellgate Bridge, and the other at Magdalene Steps in Saddler Street to monitor traffic on Elvet Bridge. Durham was the first place in the country, if not in the world, to use television for directing traffic.

The television controls in the police box, 1958. The system was officially opened by Mr G.R.H. Nugent, Parliamentary Secretary to the Ministry of Transport and Civil Aviation. The cameras were installed by Pye Ltd and the first policeman to use the new system officially was PC W. Osborne.

Durham railway station, decorated for the coronation of Queen Elizabeth in 1953. The station was designed by T. Prosser in 1857. This entrance is now the Parcel Office.

A 2–4–0 locomotive 1446 at the engine shed at Durham station in the 1920s. The driver on the right is James Maitland, father of the late Alan Maitland, who wrote many articles on Durham's history.

Gilesgate goods station, showing the old ticket office and waiting rooms, *c.* 1960s. Designed by G.T. Andrews in 1844, it is now Archibald's DIY store.

LNER drivers at Gilesgate goods station, March 1946. They are receiving their safe-driving certificates from Chief Constable Colonel Sir Eric St Johnston (in the light suit on the right). On the left in the front row is Sidney Kipling, owner of the coal-yard.

The rear of Elvet station, *c.* 1926. The old enamel advertising signs were once a common feature at stations throughout the country. They are now collectors' items, worth several hundred pounds each.

The naming ceremony for the 4–6–0 V2 locomotive 'Durham School' at Elvet station, June 1939. Gleaming like a mirror in her livery of bright apple-green, she was the second, after St Peter's York, and as it turned out the last, of a class named after northern schools. Driver Bob Hodgson and Fireman John Breeze were killed shortly afterwards on war service in France.

A North Eastern Railway horse-drawn wagon from Gilesgate goods station, waiting outside the north-bound side of Durham station in 1917. The driver is Isobel Appleby, who was doing war work because of the shortage of men during the First World War.

The Wear Valley laundry cart, 15 Claypath, *c.* 1917. The horses of this firm were stabled in Providence Row. The young boy sitting on the cart is Robert Forster.

John W. Blackburn with his father's cart in the Market Place, 1902. The occasion was the celebration of the coronation of Edward VII. Blackburn's ran a carriage business at Dragonville (West Sherburn).

This photograph came from a postcard fair in the south of England. The reverse reads: 'Rob, The Mount, Gilesgate, 1913'. The Mount is 115 Gilesgate, which was at one time owned by Mawson & Swan, yeast and egg merchants (*see* page 39).

Some of Archibald's fleet at the Goods Station yard, Gilesgate, *c.* 1949.

Mackay's carpet van, built at Fowler & Armstrong's Commercial Coachworks, Dragonville, *c.* 1960.

Arthur Wilby's chimney sweep's van, North Road, 1 June 1951. Mr Wilby had been discussing work when the handbrake failed while the van was parked. The result was as seen! Mr Wilby retired in 1984 after thirty-six years. Behind the van is the Globe cinema hall which was opened 5 May 1913.

A 1929 Rolls-Royce Phantom I hearse in Hanratty's scrapyard, Millburngate (now the site of Millburngate House), January 1961. The hearse had belonged to a Durham student but because of parking problems and complaints from neighbours, he sold it to Hanratty's.

Col. Samuel F. Cody, standing by his plane at Brandon Hill, 25 July 1911. Cody liked to be known as the son of Buffalo Bill. In 1890 he came to Europe and appeared in Wild West shows with a lady partner. They were billed as Buffalo Bill's son and daughter until Buffalo Bill himself threatened to sue. Col. Cody was the first man in Britain to fly a controlled powered plane in 1908, but he was killed in 1913 while testing a primitive seaplane.

Col. Cody's plane, Brandon Hill, 25 July 1911. He was forced to land at Pit House at 5 a.m. after suffering engine problems during a race from London to Newcastle. After a two-day delay to repair the engine and wings he set off and finished second. Local schoolchildren were given a half-day holiday to see Col. Cody and his plane.

Section Seven

Defence of the Realm

Christina Lee as Britannia at the Empire Day celebrations at Bluecoat School, Claypath, c. 1940. The first Empire Day celebrations took place in 1902.

The Marquess of Londonderry's 2nd Durham Artillery Volunteers on parade, Old Elvet, *c.* 1890. The building on the left was demolished in 1902 to make way for the Wesleyan Methodist Church (*see* page 26).

The 4th Volunteer Battalion, Durham Light Infantry (later 8th Bn, DLI), outside the main door of Durham Castle, *c.* 1900.

Durham Volunteer Artillery at the barracks (Vane Tempest Hall), *c.* 1906. Mr Thurlow is on the left of the middle row.

Durham Light Infantry cottage homes, Durham City, *c.* 1903. In 1902 a valuable site at Western Hill was presented by Mr W. Lishman, and two cottages were built on the site. The first is a memorial to Prince Christian Victor of Schleswig-Holstein, and the second is dedicated to the memory of the officers and men of the Durham Light Infantry who lost their lives in the South African War. The first occupants were Privates Coulthard and Norwood, who had both been wounded at Vaal Krantz.

Nurses at the 5th Durham Voluntary Aid Hospital, Cranmer House, North Bailey, photographed by John Edis, *c.* 1915.

The 18th, the 1st County Battalion, Durham Light Infantry (the 'Durham Pals'), part of Kitchener's new army, was raised in Durham at no cost to the nation. New recruits are seen here enlisting on the racecourse in September 1914. Most of them were clerks, tradespeople, shop assistants, students and men engaged in educational work.

The men of A Company, 18th 'Durham Pals', at Newton Hall in November 1914. They were originally stationed at Cocken Hall, but owing to the rapid increase in numbers A Company moved to Newton Hall. The Hall was built between 1717 and 1723 for Sir Henry Liddell, the attic storey being added in 1751. It was demolished in 1926.

The 'Durham Pals' on parade in Durham Market Place, 27 May 1919, before laying up the King's Colours in Durham Cathedral. Taking the salute, left, is Major D.E. Ince MC. Speeches were made from the balcony of the Town Hall by the mayor, Lord Durham, Alderman Pattison and Colonel Rowland Burdon VD, MP.

A welcome home party for soldiers returning to Grape Lane, Crossgate, after the First World War. The little boy standing in the centre at the front is Ted Sokell.

Buglers of 8th Battalion, Durham Light Infantry, Marske Camp, Redcar, 1929. Back row, left to right: ? Wright, Albert Richardson (author's great-uncle), ? Bradley, ? Rutherford, T. Carr, ? Thomas. Front row: A. Carr, ? Banks, ? Cassidy, ? Poulter.

D Crew of Durham City Observer Corps, 1939. D Crew consisted of D.C. Waller, G. Smith, J.M. Herring, C.E. Pilkington, A. Campbell, T. Darling, A. Belton, W. Davies, R. Green, W. Bowey, A.L. Parsons, R. Whinham, G. Manners, W. Surtees, W. Cunningham, J.G. Clementson, W.S. Trotter, G. Shaw, A. Almond, D. Gregory, C. Lackey and A.W. Summerbell.

A ladies' crew of Durham City Observer Corps, 14 December, 1944. At the back are Margery Gavin (left) and Daisy Armstrong; in the middle, Mary Peacock and Ernest Dixon. The front row, left to right, are: Grace Reed, Mrs Middleton, Nora Weavers, Peggy Brown, Mona Taylor, Irene Richardson, Edna Shepherd, Mary Momson. Women were allowed to join the ROC in 1941.

Durham County Council emergency ambulance, Leazes House, Claypath, 1939. On the right is Annie Laurie Stephenson (née Hopps).

Gilesgate emergency first aid post, 1939. It was based at the old Gate School at the Road Ends. Nan Salkeld from 173 Gilesgate is on the far left. On the far right is Miss L. Jacka; next to her is Miss G. Bradley, and behind her is Anna Mawson.

Durham police during the Second World War, *c*. 1940. In the centre of the middle row is Jack Raybole. In November 1940 a captured German Messerschmitt was on display in Durham Market Place as part of the War Weapons Week to raise funds.

Neville's Cross Auxiliary Fire Service, St John's Road, August 1941. The building is now a private house but at one time it was used as St John's parish hall.

Pilot Thomas ('Tommy') Keith Paul of the Royal New Zealand Air Force, photographed in 1940. He was the son of Margaret Isobelle Bone Savage who was born at Carrville, but emigrated to New Zealand in about 1913. T.K. Paul joined the New Zealand Air Force in 1939 and in 1941 returned to his roots, joining 207 Squadron, Bomber Command, RAF. On 24 May 1942 he was piloting a Lancaster bomber when it crashed on Standon Hill, Dartmoor; only two of the crew survived, Paul and the wireless operator, Tom Whitman. Two years later, on 4 January 1944, he was killed when his Wellington bomber crashed in Brockhurst Wood on Farnham Common, near Slough, Bucks. His family brought his body back to Durham City to be buried in the family grave at St Oswald's cemetery. (*See* page 8 for pictures of his grandparents.)

The grave of Tommy Paul in St Oswald's churchyard, photographed in the 1980s.

Members of the Women's Land Army from Houghall at work dredging the Wear below Pelaw Woods, between 1943 and 1947. The crane on the left was operated by Linda Shrigley, aged 19, the only woman in County Durham at that time employed on land reclamation.

The 5th Durham Scouts collecting waste paper for the war effort, photographed in New Elvet in 1943. Hatfield View can be seen in the background. In the car, from the left: Leo Sharrot, Terry Colman, -?-, -?-, Les Henry. Standing in front are Barry Dixon and Kenneth Wills.

VE Day party in Lawson Terrace, 1945. This street is situated behind the bus station in North Road.

In February 1946 an illuminated address was presented by the Town Council, together with a gift of money, to men and women from the City who served in the Forces during the Second World War. The address was designed by Mr C.R.Wheatley.

A staff party of the Durham County Press Ltd, held in the Town Hall, January 1947, to celebrate the return of staff from the war. Out of 120 staff, 50 served in the forces. Catering for the party was provided by Lyon's Café, Silver Street.

ACKNOWLEDGEMENTS

So many people have donated photographs that it is impossible to thank them individually. Institutions which have helped in various ways include: Professor Batho for writing the introduction; the History of Education Project, School of Education, Durham; Durham University Library, Palace Green; Durham City Reference Library; Durham Arts, Libraries & Museums Department; Durham County Council; Newcastle Central Library; The Trustees of the Durham Light Infantry Museum; Beamish Museum; the Taylor collection. Thanks are also due to Miss Dorothy Meade, and my wife, Norma.

Without this assistance, this book would never have been possible. If any readers have new material or information, they should contact Michael Richardson, 128 Gilesgate, Durham, DH1 1QG (0191 3841427).

BRITAIN IN OLD PHOTOGRAPHS

Aberystwyth & North Ceredigion
Around Abingdon
Acton
Alderney: A Second Selection
Along the Avon from Stratford to Tewkesbury
Altrincham
Amersham
Around Amesbury
Anglesey
Arnold & Bestwood
Arnold & Bestwood: A Second Selection
Arundel & the Arun Valley
Ashbourne
Around Ashby-de-la-Zouch
Avro Aircraft
Aylesbury
Balham & Tooting
Banburyshire
Barnes, Mortlake & Sheen
Barnsley
Bath
Beaconsfield
Bedford
Bedfordshire at Work
Bedworth
Beverley
Bexley
Bideford
Bilston
Birmingham Railways
Bishop's Stortford & Sawbridgeworth
Bishopstone & Seaford
Bishopstone & Seaford: A Second Selection
Black Country Aviation
Black Country Railways
Black Country Road Transport
Blackburn
Blackpool
Around Blandford Forum
Bletchley
Bolton
Bournemouth
Bradford
Braintree & Bocking at Work
Brecon
Brentwood
Bridgwater & the River Parrett
Bridlington
Bridport & the Bride Valley
Brierley Hill
Brighton & Hove
Brighton & Hove: A Second Selection
Bristol
Around Bristol
Brixton & Norwood
Early Broadstairs & St Peters
Bromley, Keston & Hayes

Buckingham & District
Burford
Bury
Bushbury
Camberwell
Cambridge
Cannock Yesterday & Today
Canterbury: A Second Selection
Castle Combe to Malmesbury
Chadwell Heath
Chard & Ilminster
Chatham Dockyard
Chatham & Gillingham
Cheadle
Cheam & Belmont
Chelmsford
Cheltenham: A Second Selection
Cheltenham at War
Cheltenham in the 1950s
Chepstow & the River Wye
Chesham Yesterday & Today
Cheshire Railways
Chester
Chippenham & Lacock
Chiswick
Chorley & District
Cirencester
Around Cirencester
Clacton-on-Sea
Around Clitheroe
Clwyd Railways
Clydesdale
Colchester
Colchester 1940–70
Colyton & Seaton
The Cornish Coast
Corsham & Box
The North Cotswolds
Coventry: A Second Selection
Around Coventry
Cowes & East Cowes
Crawley New Town
Around Crawley
Crewkerne & the Ham Stone Villages
Cromer
Croydon
Crystal Palace, Penge & Anerley
Darlington
Darlington: A Second Selection
Dawlish & Teignmouth
Deal
Derby
Around Devizes
Devon Aerodromes
East Devon at War
Around Didcot & the Hagbournes
Dorchester
Douglas
Dumfries
Dundee at Work
Durham People

Durham at Work
Ealing & Northfields
East Grinstead
East Ham
Eastbourne
Elgin
Eltham
Ely
Enfield
Around Epsom
Esher
Evesham to Bredon
Exeter
Exmouth & Budleigh Salterton
Fairey Aircraft
Falmouth
Farnborough
Farnham: A Second Selection
Fleetwood
Folkestone: A Second Selection
Folkestone: A Third Selection
The Forest of Dean
Frome
Fulham
Galashiels
Garsington
Around Garstang
Around Gillingham
Gloucester
Gloucester: from the Walwin Collection
North Gloucestershire at War
South Gloucestershire at War
Gosport
Goudhurst to Tenterden
Grantham
Gravesend
Around Gravesham
Around Grays
Great Yarmouth
Great Yarmouth: A Second Selection
Greenwich & Woolwich
Grimsby
Around Grimsby
Grimsby Docks
Gwynedd Railways
Hackney: A Second Selection
Hackney: A Third Selection
From Haldon to Mid-Dartmoor
Hammersmith & Shepherds Bush
Hampstead to Primrose Hill
Harrow & Pinner
Hastings
Hastings: A Second Selection
Haverfordwest
Hayes & West Drayton
Around Haywards Heath
Around Heathfield
Around Heathfield: A Second Selection
Around Helston

Around Henley-on-Thames
Herefordshire
Herne Bay
Heywood
The High Weald
The High Weald: A Second Selection
Around Highworth
Around Highworth & Faringdon
Hitchin
Holderness
Honiton & the Otter Valley
Horsham & District
Houghton-le-Spring & Hetton-le-Hole
Houghton-le-Spring & Hetton-le-Hole: A Second Selection
Huddersfield: A Second Selection
Huddersfield: A Third Selection
Ilford
Ilfracombe
Ipswich: A Second Selection
Islington
Jersey: A Third Selection
Kendal
Kensington & Chelsea
East Kent at War
Keswick & the Central Lakes
Around Keynsham & Saltford
The Changing Face of Keynsham
Kingsbridge
Kingston
Kinver
Kirkby & District
Kirkby Lonsdale
Around Kirkham
Knowle & Dorridge
The Lake Counties at Work
Lancashire
The Lancashire Coast
Lancashire North of the Sands
Lancashire Railways
East Lancashire at War
Around Lancaster
Lancing & Sompting
Around Leamington Spa
Around Leamington Spa: A Second Selection
Leeds in the News
Leeds Road & Rail
Around Leek
Leicester
The Changing Face of Leicester
Leicester at Work
Leicestershire People
Around Leighton Buzzard & Linslade
Letchworth
Lewes
Lewisham & Deptford: A Second Selection
Lichfield

Lincoln
Lincoln Cathedral
The Lincolnshire Coast
Liverpool
Around Llandudno
Around Lochaber
Theatrical London
Around Louth
The Lower Fal Estuary
Lowestoft
Luton
Lympne Airfield
Lytham St Annes
Maidenhead
Around Maidenhead
Around Malvern
Manchester
Manchester Road & Rail
Mansfield
Marlborough: A Second Selection
Marylebone & Paddington
Around Matlock
Melton Mowbray
Around Melksham
The Mendips
Merton & Morden
Middlesbrough
Midsomer Norton & Radstock
Around Mildenhall
Milton Keynes
Minehead
Monmouth & the River Wye
The Nadder Valley
Newark
Around Newark
Newbury
Newport, Isle of Wight
The Norfolk Broads
Norfolk at War
North Fylde
North Lambeth
North Walsham & District
Northallerton
Northampton
Around Norwich
Nottingham 1944–74
The Changing Face of Nottingham
Victorian Nottingham
Nottingham Yesterday & Today
Nuneaton
Around Oakham
Ormskirk & District
Otley & District
Oxford: The University
Oxford Yesterday & Today
Oxfordshire Railways: A Second Selection
Oxfordshire at School
Around Padstow
Pattingham & Wombourne

Penwith
Penzance & Newlyn
Around Pershore
Around Plymouth
Poole
Portsmouth
Poulton-le-Fylde
Preston
Prestwich
Pudsey
Radcliffe
RAF Chivenor
RAF Cosford
RAF Hawkinge
RAF Manston
RAF Manston: A Second Selection
RAF St Mawgan
RAF Tangmere
Ramsgate & Thanet Life
Reading
Reading: A Second Selection
Redditch & the Needle District
Redditch: A Second Selection
Richmond, Surrey
Rickmansworth
Around Ripley
The River Soar
Romney Marsh
Romney Marsh: A Second Selection
Rossendale
Around Rotherham
Rugby
Around Rugeley
Ruislip
Around Ryde
St Albans
St Andrews
Salford
Salisbury
Salisbury: A Second Selection
Salisbury: A Third Selection
Around Salisbury
Sandhurst & Crowthorne
Sandown & Shanklin
Sandwich
Scarborough
Scunthorpe
Seaton, Lyme Regis & Axminster
Around Seaton & Sidmouth
Sedgley & District
The Severn Vale
Sherwood Forest
Shrewsbury
Shrewsbury: A Second Selection
Shropshire Railways
Skegness
Around Skegness
Skipton & the Dales
Around Slough

Smethwick
Somerton & Langport
Southampton
Southend-on-Sea
Southport
Southwark
Southwell
Southwold to Aldeburgh
Stafford
Around Stafford
Staffordshire Railways
Around Staveley
Stepney
Stevenage
The History of Stilton Cheese
Stoke-on-Trent
Stoke Newington
Stonehouse to Painswick
Around Stony Stratford
Around Stony Stratford: A Second Selection
Stowmarket
Streatham
Stroud & the Five Valleys
Stroud & the Five Valleys: A Second Selection
Stroud's Golden Valley
The Stroudwater and Thames & Severn Canals
The Stroudwater and Thames & Severn Canals: A Second Selection
Suffolk at Work
Suffolk at Work: A Second Selection
The Heart of Suffolk
Sunderland
Sutton
Swansea
Swindon: A Third Selection
Swindon: A Fifth Selection
Around Tamworth
Taunton
Around Taunton
Teesdale
Teesdale: A Second Selection
Tenbury Wells
Around Tettenhall & Codshall
Tewkesbury & the Vale of Gloucester
Thame to Watlington
Around Thatcham
Around Thirsk
Thornbury to Berkeley
Tipton
Around Tonbridge
Trowbridge
Around Truro
TT Races
Tunbridge Wells

Tunbridge Wells: A Second Selection
Twickenham
Uley, Dursley & Cam
The Upper Fal
The Upper Tywi Valley
Uxbridge, Hillingdon & Cowley
The Vale of Belvoir
The Vale of Conway
Ventnor
Wakefield
Wallingford
Walsall
Waltham Abbey
Wandsworth at War
Wantage, Faringdon & the Vale Villages
Around Warwick
Weardale
Weardale: A Second Selection
Wednesbury
Wells
Welshpool
West Bromwich
West Wight
Weston-super-Mare
Around Weston-super-Mare
Weymouth & Portland
Around Wheatley
Around Whetstone
Whitchurch to Market Drayton
Around Whitstable
Wigton & the Solway Plain
Willesden
Around Wilton
Wimbledon
Around Windsor
Wingham, Addisham & Littlebourne
Wisbech
Witham & District
Witney
Around Witney
The Witney District
Wokingham
Around Woodbridge
Around Woodstock
Woolwich
Woolwich Royal Arsenal
Around Wootton Bassett, Cricklade & Purton
Worcester
Worcester in a Day
Around Worcester
Worcestershire at Work
Around Worthing
Wotton-under-Edge to Chipping Sodbury
Wymondham & Attleborough
The Yorkshire Wolds